DATE DUE

FOLLETT

MEMORIAL MEDIA CENTER

1331342 BC MAT
5 Seconds of Summer

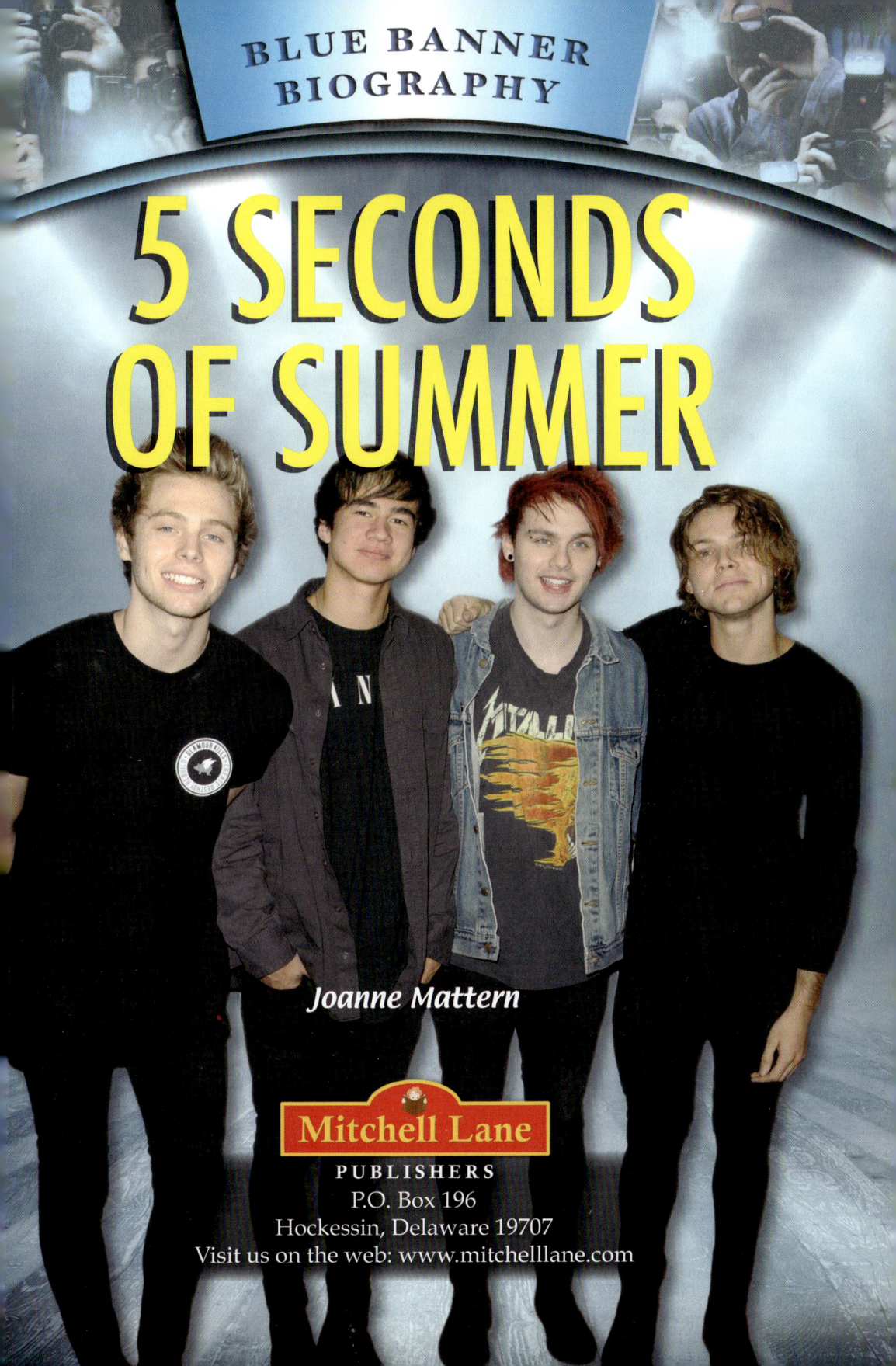

BLUE BANNER BIOGRAPHY

5 SECONDS OF SUMMER

Joanne Mattern

Mitchell Lane
PUBLISHERS
P.O. Box 196
Hockessin, Delaware 19707
Visit us on the web: www.mitchelllane.com

Copyright © 2016 by Mitchell Lane Publishers, Inc. All rights reserved. No part of this book may be reproduced without written permission from the publisher. Printed and bound in the United States of America.

Printing   1   2   3   4   5   6   7   8   9

Blue Banner Biographies

5 Seconds of Summer	Ice Cube	Miguel Tejada
Abby Wambach	Ja Rule	Mike Trout
Adele	Jamie Foxx	Nancy Pelosi
Alicia Keys	Jason Derulo	Natasha Bedingfield
Allen Iverson	Jay-Z	Nicki Minaj
Ashanti	Jennifer Hudson	One Direction
Ashlee Simpson	Jennifer Lopez	Orianthi
Ashton Kutcher	Jessica Simpson	Orlando Bloom
Avril Lavigne	JJ Watt	P. Diddy
Blake Lively	J. K. Rowling	Peyton Manning
Blake Shelton	Joe Flacco	Pharrell Williams
Bow Wow	John Legend	Pink
Brett Favre	Justin Berfield	Pit Bull
Britney Spears	Justin Timberlake	Prince William
Bruno Mars	Kanye West	Queen Latifah
CC Sabathia	Kate Hudson	Rihanna
Carrie Underwood	Katy Perry	Robert Downey Jr.
Chris Brown	Keith Urban	Robert Pattinson
Chris Daughtry	Kelly Clarkson	Ron Howard
Christina Aguilera	Kenny Chesney	Russell Wilson
Ciara	Ke$ha	Sean Kingston
Clay Aiken	Kevin Durant	Selena
Cole Hamels	Kristen Stewart	Shakira
Condoleezza Rice	Lady Gaga	Shia LaBeouf
Corbin Bleu	Lance Armstrong	Shontelle Layne
Daniel Radcliffe	Leona Lewis	Soulja Boy Tell 'Em
David Ortiz	Lil Wayne	Stephenie Meyer
David Wright	Lionel Messi	Taylor Swift
Derek Jeter	Lindsay Lohan	T.I.
Drew Brees	LL Cool J	Timbaland
Dwayne Wade	Luke Bryan	Tim McGraw
Eminem	Ludacris	Tim Tebow
Eve	Mariah Carey	Toby Keith
Fergie	Mario	Usher
Flo Rida	Mary J. Blige	Vanessa Anne Hudgens
Gwen Stefani	Mary-Kate and Ashley Olsen	Will.i.am
Hope Solo	Megan Fox	Zac Efron

Library of Congress Cataloging-in-Publication Data
Mattern, Joanne, 1963–
 5 Seconds of Summer / by Joanne Mattern.
   pages cm. — (Blue banner biographies)
 Includes bibliographical references and index.
 ISBN 978-1-68020-089-8 (library bound)
1. 5 Seconds of Summer (Musical group)—Juvenile literature. 2. Rock musicians—Australia—Biography—Juvenile literature. I. Title. II. Title: Five Seconds of Summer.

ML3930.A12M37 2015
782.42166092′2—dc23
[B]

2015012931

eBook ISBN: 978-1-68020-090-4

ABOUT THE AUTHOR: Joanne Mattern first learned about 5 Seconds of Summer thanks to her daughter Leanne, who is a big fan of the band and of alternative rock music. Leanne assisted with the research on this book, which made it a family team effort. Mattern has written many celebrity biographies for Mitchell Lane Publishers, including books about One Direction, Jennifer Hudson, Blake Lively, and Ludacris. She lives in New York State with her husband, four children, and several pets.

PUBLISHER'S NOTE: This story has not been authorized or endorsed by 5 Seconds of Summer.

Blue Banner Biography

Chapter 1
Famous Fans 5

Chapter 2
Growing Up 9

Chapter 3
Rough Beginnings 13

Chapter 4
The Road to the Top 19

Chapter 5
Music and More 25

Chronology 30

Discography 30

Further Reading 31

Works Consulted 31

Index 32

Guitarist Michael Clifford is known for his ever-changing, brightly dyed hair. Here he rocks orange hair as he performs at the 2014 iHeart Radio Music Festival in Las Vegas.

Famous Fans

Calum Hood, Luke Hemmings, Ashton Irwin, and Michael Clifford were just four music-loving teenagers living in the suburbs of Sydney, Australia. Like many teens, the friends decided to form a band, but there weren't many opportunities to play in local concert halls, so they turned to social media to find new fans.

Hood, Hemmings, Irwin, and Clifford named their band 5 Seconds of Summer (5SOS). They began making simple music videos and posting them on YouTube. At first they posted cover songs (when a band performs a song by another artist). 5 Seconds of Summer's covers included music by pop stars, but also songs by alternative rock bands such as Blink-182 and Mayday Parade.

At first, only the band's friends and family watched the videos, but then more and more people discovered them. In July 2011, 5 Seconds of Summer posted a cover for "Next to You" by Chris Brown and Justin Bieber. The video took off, earning more than six hundred thousand views on YouTube. Still, the band was pretty much unknown, especially to people outside of the Sydney, Australia area.

In May 2012, 5 Seconds of Summer posted another video. This time it was a song they wrote called "Gotta Get Out." The video was simple—just the four band members singing. Many people watched the video after it was posted to YouTube. One of those viewers would change 5 Seconds of Summer's lives forever.

Louis Tomlinson is a member of the popular band One Direction. After he watched the video, he posted a link to it on Twitter with the message, "Been a fan of this band for a while, everyone get behind them." Tomlinson had more than seventeen million Twitter followers, and they were eager to check out the band he liked so much. "Gotta Get Out" received millions of views, and then people all over the world began talking about 5 Seconds of Summer.

5 Seconds of Summer first became famous in their home country of Australia. Australian fans show their love before the band's concert at the Palais Theatre in Melbourne on May 3, 2014.

One Direction's Niall Horan gave 5 Seconds of Summer a good push when 5SOS released their video, "Out of My Limit" in November 2012. Horan tweeted his love for the song along with a link to the video. Once again, millions of fans rushed to YouTube to check out the song.

The link between the two bands became even stronger when One Direction invited 5 Seconds of Summer to be the opening band on One Direction's worldwide tour in 2013. 5SOS toured with One Direction again in 2014 and also later signed with One Direction's management company.

Today 5 Seconds of Summer is tremendously popular around the world. While they may owe their original success to One Direction, 5 Seconds of Summer are very different from their friends in that popular band.

Drummer Ashton Irwin happily poses with fans at the 28th Annual ARIA Awards in Sydney on November 24, 2014. The ARIAs are similar to the People's Choice Awards in the United States.

Luke Hemmings and Calum Hood face off during the 2014 iHeart Radio Music Festival in Las Vegas on September 20, 2014. The concert was broadcast all over the world on TV and the Internet.

Growing Up

The four members of 5 Seconds of Summer may be worldwide superstars now, but they certainly didn't start out that way. All of the members come from modest beginnings in the working-class neighborhoods of Plumpton, Quakers Hill, and Riverstone.

Luke Robert Hemmings, the youngest member of the band, was born on July 16, 1996, in Sydney, Australia. His father, Andrew, was a pool repairman, and his mother, Liz, was a math teacher. Luke has two older brothers, Ben and Jack. "Our beginnings were so humble," he told *People* magazine. "I grew up in a small house in the middle of nowhere." No one in the family showed an interest in music. But when Luke was ten years old he discovered Good Charlotte's album, *The Young and the Hopeless*. "I think I bought it because the album cover was cool," Hemmings told *Alternative Press* magazine. "That was my favorite album for a long time." And then Hemmings discovered Green Day, a popular American rock band.

One thing led to another — one of Hemmings' older brothers had a guitar, and he taught Hemmings to play a few simple songs. Soon Hemmings was playing four hours a day and learning songs by many different artists. Hemmings also studied music when he was a student at Norwest Christian College.

Michael Gordon Clifford was born on November 20, 1995, in Sydney, Australia. He is the only child of Karen and Daryl Clifford, who ran a computer business. Clifford soon became known for his rebellious personality. He was constantly getting into trouble at Norwest Christian College for not wearing the proper socks according to the school's uniform code. Clifford has admitted that school was "torture" for him and he often cut classes. He told the *Daily Mail* that he "got a D in music" even though he was quickly becoming an excellent guitar player. "I started playing *Guitar Hero* when I was 9 or 10, and that got me into older music," he explained to *Alternative Press*.

Calum Thomas Hood was born in Sydney, Australia, on January 25, 1996. His mother, Joy, is from New Zealand and his father, David, is Scottish. Hood has an older sister named Mali Koa, who is also a singer and songwriter. Hood enjoyed music, but he grew up thinking that he wanted to be a professional soccer player. He seemed much too shy to be a rock star. "Calum is a massively shy guy, but he's come out of his shell a bit," bandmate Clifford told *People* magazine in 2014. Hood agreed, explaining that his parents were shocked when he joined the band. "It was weird for them because they didn't know I really liked music. I was always the sporty one."

Hood and Clifford both attended Norwest Christian College and were good friends. They met Hemmings at school later, but the boys did not hit it off right away. "Michael didn't like Luke at first, and I was best friends with Michael at that time, so I actually didn't like him [Luke Hemmings]," Hood explained in a video the band posted online. "But in the back of my mind I was like, 'He seems like a really cool guy.'"

Hemmings had begun posting music videos online and when Clifford heard about them and found out that Hemmings was also a fan of Green Day, his opinion of Hemmings changed. "Somehow . . . we became best friends," Clifford said. Soon afterward, the three boys started the band.

Ashton Fletcher Irwin was the last member to join the band. He was born on July 7, 1994, in Hornsby, Australia, making him the oldest member of the group. His American father left the family when Irwin was just two years old. Irwin grew up with his mother Anne Marie and two younger siblings Lauren and Harry. Unlike the other members of the band, Irwin enjoyed music at an early age. His uncle and his stepfather were both drummers in local bands. Irwin started playing the drums after he saw a video of Green Day's drummer. Irwin and several school friends formed a band at Richmond High School, which was about twenty minutes away from Norwest Christian College. Still, Irwin didn't feel like he fit in at school. "I was a loner doing musical things on my own," he said. Being teased affected him deeply, and to this day he often speaks out against bullying.

Because Irwin went to a different school, the other members of 5 Seconds of Summer didn't know him that well. All that would change when 5 Seconds of Summer needed help from a friend to take advantage of a big opportunity.

Ashton Irwin enjoys a traditional slime bath after the band's performance at Nickelodeon's Kids' Choice Awards on March 28, 2015.

Rough Beginnings

Hemmings, Clifford, and Hood came together as a band in 2011 when they were about fifteen years old. They decided on the name 5 Seconds of Summer after brainstorming (creative problem solving) possible band names during school.

Hemmings created a YouTube channel and the band started posting videos on YouTube. The videos weren't very good—in fact, Hemmings once described them as "awful." However, they attracted the attention of several people in the local music scene.

Adam Wilkinson became 5SOS's manager after he met the band at Sydney's Studio 301 in November 2011. "They just had this nervous energy that really excited me," he explained to *People* magazine. That same month, the manager of Sydney's Annandale Hotel sent a message to the band's Facebook page, inviting them to perform at the hotel. Hemmings, Clifford, and Hood were thrilled. The Annandale Hotel was a well-known club where many famous rock bands had played.

There was just one problem—the band did not have a drummer. Clifford reached out to his friend, Irwin, who he knew through mutual friends. "Michael sort of over-exaggerated," Ashton told *USA Today* in April 2014. Clifford had told Ashton about two hundred people would be there, but "We went onstage and there were twelve people there." Irwin says that performance was his favorite because "it was so new to us. It was a terrible gig, but there was just something about it that me and the boys [sic] loved. We knew it was the start of something cool for us."

The boys threw themselves into rehearsing, even though their musical instruments and recording efforts weren't the best. Hood did not have a bass guitar at first, so he strummed the low E string on a regular guitar. They recorded videos with an iPhone mounted on a microphone stand. They even rehearsed in the dark in order to feel completely confident in their playing. "We thought if we can't see what we are doing and we can still play, then we might sound good when the lights are turned on," Irwin explained.

Their hard work paid off, and soon 5 Seconds of Summer were touring around Australia. That was not easy—all of the members were still in school and had to keep up with classes and exams. Irwin sometimes snuck his bandmates out of school, picking them up in his car and driving them to concerts. The band had some trouble fitting

> **Clifford had told Ashton about two hundred people would be there, but "We went onstage and there were twelve people there." Irwin says that performance was his favorite.**

in with the Sydney rock scene. "People hated us," Irwin recalled to the *Canberra Times* in 2014. "They told us we were bad every single day . . . But you have to suck at the beginning and you have to have crap for instruments and not be able to afford stuff and work from the bottom for the band to grow."

Sydney's underground rock fans might not have liked 5 Seconds of Summer, but millions of fans on YouTube certainly did. In recent years social media has become increasingly important in introducing new bands to the world. As Irwin told musictakeabow.com, "You can build a fan base now before you've actually released anything, so it's all quite weird. Whereas before we'd be touring our butts off for years, but that's not the only way that you can build a fan base, which is nice."

5 Seconds of Summer talks to the press at the 2014 iHeart Radio Festival in Las Vegas. The band is known for their goofy behavior. Michael Clifford has been known to stick out his tongue.

15

Record company executives were also taking note of 5 Seconds of Summer's increasing popularity. In August 2012, the band signed a contract with Sony ATV Music Publishing. They also went into Sydney's Studio 301 to record an EP titled *Unplugged*. (An EP is an extended play disc that contains fewer songs than a full-length music album.) The band was stunned when the EP reached number three on Australia's iTunes chart and the Top 20 in New Zealand and Sweden. Another bright moment occurred when 5SOS was asked to be the opening band for Hot Chelle Rae's Australian tour in 2012.

After the Hot Chelle Rae tour ended, Hemmings, Clifford, Hood, and Irwin teamed up with Joel Chapman and Christian Lo Russo from the Australian band Amy Meredith to write some of the songs on the next 5 Seconds of Summer EP, *Somewhere New*. Chapman also produced the EP, which was released in November 2012.

In December, 5 Seconds of Summer flew to London to write music with several well-known alternative rock musicians. "It was a massive learning curve," Hemmings admitted. "To be thrown into the deep end like that . . . I think that's how we've done most things in this band." The boys were thrilled to meet and work with their musical idols Benji and Joel Madden from Good Charlotte and Alex Gaskarth from the band All Time Low. "I never thought I'd be friends with those guys," Clifford

> The band was stunned when the EP reached number three on Australia's iTunes chart and the Top 20 in New Zealand and Sweden.

Michael Clifford and Luke Hemmings perform during a December 2014 concert in San Jose, California. The band's sound features very loud and energetic guitars.

admitted to *Alternative Press*. The Madden brothers returned the love, telling *People* magazine that 5 Seconds of Summer reminded them "of a young Good Charlotte, and we love seeing them carry on the message and sounds that GC did so many years ago."

By the end of 2012 One Direction had introduced 5 Seconds of Summer to their fan base. Soon afterward One Direction approached 5SOS with an offer they couldn't refuse—even though they came close to saying no.

Left to Right: Luke Robert Hemmings, Michael Clifford, Calum Hood, and Ashton Irwin. The iHeart Radio broadcast featured many different popular recording artists.

The Road to the Top

Early in 2013 the members of 5 Seconds of Summer received an incredible offer. One Direction's management asked them if they wanted to be the opening act for One Direction's worldwide tour to support their new album *Take Me Home*. 5SOS would be performing all over Australia, the United Kingdom, and the United States, including sold-out shows in large arenas.

The members of the band weren't sure opening for One Direction was a good idea. "We weren't sure if it would work that well," Hemmings told *Alternative Press* magazine in 2014. "I think we'd only done, like, sixteen shows at that point." The bigger problem was that One Direction was a popular boy band, and 5 Seconds of Summer just didn't see themselves the same way. "We thought we were really, *really* different than One Direction," Hemmings explained. "They had a really dedicated fan base—were they going to hate us? We definitely didn't want to be called the Australian 1D." Clifford also didn't like the idea of touring with One Direction. He was hoping the band would be invited to join the 2013 Vans Warped Tour, a summer-long festival that brings a large number of pop punk, metal, and alternative rock bands to cities all over the United States.

It was Irwin who finally convinced the band that the 1D connection was a good idea. "We just saw the boy-band thing and thought, 'That's not who we are; why would we want to go on tour with them?'" he explained to *Alternative Press*. "But I'm the bigger-picture guy in the band. You know, if you do *this*, it can lead to *that* down the road. I was like, 'Dudes, these are *arenas*. It's 20,000 people a night for a year.' They were afraid of us getting labeled the next One Direction. And I was like, 'Yeah, but if they come see us live, they'll realize that's not the case.'"

> "They were afraid of us getting labeled the next One Direction. And I was like, 'Yeah, but if they come see us live, they'll realize that's not the case.'" said Irwin.

Irwin's argument won over the rest of the band, and 5 Seconds of Summer spent most of 2013 on tour with One Direction. Hemmings was only sixteen when the tour started, so his mother Liz went with them. Liz loved watching her son and his friends perform. "It makes me tear up every time," she admitted to *People* magazine. "I've seen hundreds of shows, and each one—it doesn't matter if it's a tiny little venue or Wembley Stadium—I get the same feeling of pride." The tour was a success and the members of One Direction and 5 Seconds of Summer became fast friends. The two bands got along so well that 5 Seconds of Summer toured with One Direction again on their 2014 *Where We Are* world tour, and 1D's

5 Seconds of Summer made many new fans when they performed as the opening act for One Direction during 2013 and 2014. Here, Luke Hemmings excites the crowd during a 2014 show.

Modest Management began handling 5 Seconds of Summer's business as well.

After the 2013 tour ended, 5 Seconds of Summer signed with Capitol Records and went into the studio to record their first album. Meanwhile, they released several more EPs and singles. "She Looks So Perfect" was released in March 2014 and became a hit in the United States. It was also a number-one hit in the United Kingdom, as was their second single "Don't Stop."

On June 27, 5SOS released their first full-length album *5 Seconds of Summer* in Europe and Australia. The album was released in the United States in July. It entered the *Billboard* chart at number one and reached number one in

The band poses happily with covers of their hit single, "She Looks So Perfect," at a celebration outside Capitol Records in March 2015.

Music is just part of the fun at a 5SOS concert. The stage also features elaborate and colorful lights and displays.

thirteen other countries. The album also won the Best International Newcomer Award from *Kerrang!*, a British rock magazine, and that was a thrill for the band. During 2014, 5 Seconds of Summer received six World Music Awards nominations and three MTV Italy Awards nominations. Their song "Don't Stop" won an MTV Video Music Award for Best Lyric Video.

5 Seconds of Summer seemed to be all over American television during the summer of 2014. They made their first US television appearance at the *Billboard Music Awards* in May, but one of their biggest appearances was on the *Today* show on July 22. Fans began lining up six days before the live broadcast, and weatherman Al Roker announced, "This is probably the biggest crowd we've ever had." 5 Seconds of Summer had arrived at the top of the music world.

Luke Hemmings leans into the crowd during a concert. The band has a special connection with their fans, who are called the 5SOS Fam.

Music and More

During 2014, 5 Seconds of Summer took a big step that would give them more control over their music and their careers. They started their own record label, Hi Or Hey Records, a part of Capitol Records. The band's first album was released on Hi Or Hey, and they announced that 5SOS would release future albums on the label as well. "We have created this label for you guys," they announced to the band's fans on their Website. "We have achieved so much together over the last two years and if it were not for you, we don't know where we would be . . . Hi Or Hey Records means we can stay in control of our career. Things have gone pretty well with you and us running the show so we want to keep it that way."

The band has big plans for 2015 to tour the world again during the spring and summer, this time headlining their own tour called *Rock Out with Your Socks Out*. Although the band had headlined small tours before, this will be their first major world tour. After releasing the live album *LiveSOS* at the end of 2014, the band also plans to go back into the studio and record music for a new album.

Members of 5 Seconds of Summer leap into the air while performing at KIIS-FM's Jingle Ball concert at the Staples Center in Los Angeles on December 5, 2014.

The band also does charity work. In 2013 Hemmings, Clifford, Hood, and Irwin supported the charity Books to Build On, which sends books to needy communities. After several schools were destroyed in a tornado in Moore, Oklahoma, the charity provided thousands of books to help those schools rebuild their libraries.

The band has promoted a charity called To Write Love on Her Arms, or TWLOHA. This American charity helps teenagers who struggle with depression, addiction, and thoughts of suicide by providing information and connecting teens with treatment sites so they can find help. 5 Seconds of Summer promoted the charity by wearing T-shirts and other merchandise with the charity's logo. In April 2013 Hood posted a photo of himself wearing a TWLOHA shirt and tweeted, "One thing I feel real passionate about. Check them out! #MakeADifference."

5 Seconds of Summer loves their fans, known as the 5SOS Fam (family). As Clifford told the *Daily Telegraph*, "When your whole career is based around other people supporting you, being grateful about everything they have done for you is the most important thing, other than the music." The 5SOS Fam is extremely loyal and will quickly defend the band if anyone puts down the band's music.

Many of 5 Seconds of Summer's fans are teenage girls. The reason for this is because of the band's link with One Direction, whose fan base is largely made up of young girls. Also 5 Seconds of Summer has four good-looking young men. Because of this many critics call 5 Seconds of Summer a "boy band" and refuse to take them seriously. 5SOS is quick to argue that they are not a boy band at all. Unlike most boy bands, they write their own music and play their own instruments.

5 Seconds of Summer has had musical influences from bands that play punk, hard rock, and alternative rock. "As far as our vision goes, all we've ever wanted to do is to be seen as bringing back guitars," Clifford told *Alternative Press*. "We are quite a confusing band . . . If a band like All Time Low got bigger from our success, that would be incredible . . . A band like that is the reason I'm playing music." Indeed, many alternative rock and punk bands, such as All Time Low, have great respect for 5 Seconds of Summer. Irwin told *USA*

> *"When your whole career is based around other people supporting you, being grateful about everything they have done for you is the most important thing, other than the music,"* said Clifford.

Today, "I don't care what people call us, as long as we're making the music we love."

In 2014 music critic Miles Raymer stated that "Like It Or Not, 5 Seconds of Summer is Rock's Future," on www.chicagoreader.com. It is a responsibility being labeled the future of rock music, but 5SOS seem willing to take up the challenge. Irwin told *Alternative Press*, "I really like when people say we're not meant to be here or we're not meant to do this. I think challenging people is the smartest thing a band can do. It means you're doing something different." And being different is one thing 5 Seconds of Summer is happy to do.

5 Seconds of Summer performed several concerts as part of the Jingle Ball tour in December 2014. Here members of the band rock out during a concert in Washington, D.C.

Left to Right: Calum, Ashton, Luke, and Michael backstage during the Jingle Ball show at the Staples Center on December 5, 2014.

CHRONOLOGY

1994	Ashton Irwin is born on July 7.
1995	Michael Clifford is born on November 20.
1996	Calum Hood is born on January 25. Luke Hemmings is born on July 16.
2011	Luke Hemmings, Michael Clifford, and Calum Hood form 5 Seconds of Summer, they post videos on YouTube and they invite Ashton Irwin to join the band before a performance at Sydney's Annandale Hotel.
2012	Members of the band One Direction notice several of 5 Seconds of Summer's videos. 5 Seconds of Summer signs a publishing deal with Sony ATV Music Publishing. 5SOS record their first EP, *Unplugged*. 5SOS tours with Hot Chelle Rae, they record their second EP, *Somewhere New*, and they fly to London to write music.
2013	5 Seconds of Summer opens for One Direction on their world tour.
2014	5 Seconds of Summer starts their own record label, Hi Or Hey Records and they open again for One Direction on their world tour. 5SOS's first single "She Looks So Perfect" debuts at number one on the *Billboard* charts. They release EPs *She Looks So Perfect, Don't Stop, Amnesia,* and *Good Girls*. 5SOS releases its first album, *5 Seconds of Summer*.
2015	5SOS headlines its first world tour.

DISCOGRAPHY

2012	*Unplugged (EP)*		**2014**	*Amnesia (EP)*
2012	*Somewhere New (EP)*		**2014**	*Good Girls (EP)*
2014	*She Looks So Perfect (EP)*		**2014**	*5 Seconds of Summer*
2014	*Don't Stop (EP)*		**2014**	*LiveSOS*

PHOTO CREDITS: Cover, p. 1—INB/Ivan Nikolov/WENN/Newscom, (background)—Thinkstock; pp. 4, 15—Kobby Dagan/Dreamstime.com; p. 6—Graham Denholm/Getty Images; p. 7—Ryan Pierse/Getty Images; p. 8—Kobby Dagan/Dreamstime.com; p. 12—Tommaso Boddi/WireImage/Getty Images; p. 17—Tim Mosenfelder/Getty Images; p. 18—Press Line Photos/Splash News/Newscom; p. 21—Jeff Kravitz/OneD; p. 22—Lester Cohen/WireImage; p. 23—Jeff Kravitz/OneD/Getty Images; p. 24—Jeff Kravitz FilmMagic, Inc.; p. 26—Jason Merritt/Getty Images; p. 28—C Flanigan/FilmMagic/Getty Images; p. 29—2014 HPA/Hutchins Photo/Newscom.

Further Reading

Archer, Mandy, and Stephanie Clarkson. *5 Seconds of Summer: Shoot for the Stars*. New York: Scholastic, 2014.

Boone, Mary. *5 Seconds of Summer: She Looks So Perfect*. Chicago: Triumph Books, 2014.

Croft, Malcolm. *5 Seconds of Summer: The Ultimate Fan Book*. Hauppauge, NY: Barron's Educational Series, 2014.

Works Consulted

"All About 5 Seconds of Summer. *People* Collector's Special." *People* Magazine. October 2014.

5 Seconds of Summer. *Hey, Let's Make a Band*. New York: HarperCollins Publishers, 2014.

Lucy, Evan. "Why Pop Punk Needs 5 Seconds of Summer." *Alternative Press*, August 2014, 89-100.

Raymer, Miles. "Like It Or Not, 5 Seconds of Summer is Rock's Future." ChicagoReader.com, April 29, 2014. http://www.chicagoreader.com/Bleader/archives/2014/04/29/like-it-or-not-5-seconds-of-summer-is-rocks-future

Ryan, Patrick. "Meet the Boys of 5 Seconds of Summer." USA Today.com. April 20, 2014. http://www.usatoday.com/story/life/music/2014/04/20/on-the-verge-five-seconds-of-summer/7611321/

Shedden, Iain and Mitchell Nadin. "Sydney teens hit the big time as 5SOS storms the world of pop." *The Australian*. April 12, 2014. http://www.theaustralian.com.au/arts/music/sydney-teens-hit-the-big-time-as-5sos-storms-the-world-of-pop/story-fn9d2mxu-1226881420498?nk=24d4019d0a3dab9ffde3b1573c5b2b59

On the Internet

5 Seconds of Summer
   http://www.5sos.com
5 SOS Online
   http://www.5sosonline.com

INDEX

5 Seconds of Summer (album) 22
5SOS Fam 27
All Time Low 16, 27-28
Annandale Hotel 13-14
Billboard 22
Billboard Music Awards 23
Books to Build On 26
Capitol Records 22, 25
Clifford, Michael 5, 10, 11, 13, 14, 27
"Don't Stop" 22, 23
Gaskarth, Alex 16
Good Charlotte 16, 17
"Gotta Get Out" 6
Green Day 9, 11
Hemmings, Liz 9, 20
Hemmings, Luke 5, 9-10, 11, 13, 20
Hi or Hey Records 25
Hood, Calum 5, 10, 11, 13, 26-27
Horan, Niall 7
Hot Chelle Rae 16
Irwin, Ashton 5, 11, 14, 20
iTunes 16
LiveSOS 25
Madden, Benji 16, 17

Madden, Joel 16, 17
Modest Management 20
MTV 23
"Next to You" 5
Norwest Christian College 10, 11
One Direction 6, 7, 17, 19-20, 27
"Out of My Limit" 7
Raymer, Miles 28
Richmond High School 11
Rock Out with Your Socks Out 25
Roker, Al 23
"She Looks So Perfect" 22
Somewhere New 16
Sony ATV Music 16
Sydney, Australia 5, 13, 15
To Write Love on Her Arms (TWLOHA) 26
Today Show, The 23
Tomlinson, Louis 6
Twitter 6
Unplugged 16
Vans Warped Tour 19-20
Wilkinson, Adam 13
YouTube 5-6, 7, 13, 15